Straight from the Heart

Straight from the Heart

Jagmit Singh

DIGITALSPINES

First Edition, 2023

Paperback ISBN: 978-81-977702-9-6
eBook ISBN: 978-81-19316-03-8
WebPDF ISBN: 978-81-19316-05-2

Published by DIGITAL SPINES.
Originally published by 16Leaves.

I dedicate this book to my grandfather, (Bauji,)S Indar Singh jee and my parents S. Pritam Singh jee and Mrs Vidushi Pritam Singh.

Though they are no more physically with us, their blessings will always be with me.

I am what I am all because of them and I am sure they would be proud that I wrote a book.

I would like to thank my immediate family, Preeti, my wife, Arshiya my daughter and Naunidh my son in law and my sisters Jasleen and Manjula for their support and encouragement. A special mention to my cousin Puneet for motivating me.

My thanks also to my close friends from college (SRCC, New Delhi) Denzil and Chandan.

Special thanks to friends Ambassador Manjeev S Puri and his wife Namrita.

I would like to thank my entire batch of Modern School (The Together Forever 1976!)

In particular Radhika, Nita, Dr Harsh, Deepak Rana and Pradeep Bahl.

My entire group of Table Tennis friends from Saket Sports Complex New Delhi.

I cannot forget to thank all my Facebook Friends and Air India Colleagues too for their constant encouragement. Ambassador Deepa Gopalan Wadhwa and (Juju Chachiji) Mrs Jyotsana Singh for always appreciating my attempts at poetry.

A special thanks to Cecil and Darlene for their encouragement and support.

Most of all my thanks and gratitude to Almighty God as everything is possible only with His grace and blessings.

CONTENTS

1.

Zero

Many years ago...
It is said... An Indian invented zero...

So beautiful it is... Round shaped.
A circle. With no beginning or end.

Reminding us of God.
Who has no end or beginning!
Round like the earth. The planets
And the sun.
Like the balls. Tennis. Golf
And all.
Like the molecules. Atoms.
Et all.

Talking of God. Infinite.
Present in all. Everywhere and in everything.
Big or small. In the smallest too.
And as we go. Smaller and smaller.
We reach almost nothing. Or zero.
So God is in nothing too.

In fact. If we can. Remove or reduce.
The I (pronounced eye) in ourselves.
Make our ego. Smaller and smaller.
That is a sure way.
To find God

We think we are very big.
Actually we are quite small.
Or nothing at all.
If we realize this.
That's not a bad thing!

So try and be like zero.
For zero is quite a Hero!

2.

Zakham

Log to Yun hee samajhte hain
Ki mein khairyat mein hoon
Inhey kya maloom
Seene mein Kitna dard chhupa Hai!

Dikhney mein to mein
Theek thaak lagta hun
Magar jo dil mein dard hai
Uskee marham kiskey paas Hai?

Koi doctor key paas
Isska ilaaj naheen
Uska dard to ab bus
Kabr kee intezar karta Hai!

Kabhi kabhee to yeh dard
Accha lagta hai
Agar yeh thokar nahee lagee hoti
To phir zindagi ka maksad kya tha

Kai dost to chale gaye
Is zindagi key khel ko chhod ke
Unkee yaadon ke saharon se
Ab zindagi se ladai ladnee hogi!

3. Amazing

Never cease to wonder,
That we are here,
And can see and feel,
All this beauty!

Isn't it amazing,
That this globe,
Which is twirling around,
Moving speedily across space,
And we don't feel a thing!

Millions of people,
All looking different,
Yet sometimes,
He makes them look alike!

Brilliant is His brush,
Amazing His creativity,
Some he gives mansions,
Others a little less.

He is a Master,
He knows what He's doing,
And does what He wants!

Some He makes,
Who live in water forever,
And some who can fly!
Isn't it amazing!!

Just look around,
Feel His presence,
The beauty on this earth,
And the vastness of the sky,
And the Universe!!
Isn't it amazing!
Isn't it Amazing!!

4.

Who Am I

I am so small,
I know nought,
If I remember Him,
I need nothing else.

Nothing to prove,
No need to say,
Just bliss and bliss,
Everywhere.

Accept what is happening,
He makes it happen,
No need to fear,
For He is everywhere.

Just think of Him,
Take his name,
Aloud or in your mind,
Then you will need nothing.

It is His will,
If He gives me the understanding,
If He gives me the faith,
Then I need nothing else,
I am complete, with His grace.

5.

We Messed It Up

We made these countries,
These divisions and boundaries,
God made the world,
But we messed it up!

We made the castes,
The untouchables and the like,
God had made the human race,
But we messed it up!

We made the religions,
And said mine is better than yours,
And fought so many wars,
Truly we messed it up!

We made the weapons and bombs,
We killed so many innocents,
God had given us life to enjoy,
But we messed it up!

We cut off all the trees,
We succumbed to our greed,
We polluted the skies,

The rivers and the oceans,
We've made a big mess!

Can we learn,
We are so far, the only one of our kind,
Are we here to hate each other,
Or to prove a point.

Let's live in peace and harmony,
Let's learn from the animals,
They eat only as much as required,
They don't wage wars on each other,
They don't hoard and cheat.

Let's leave the future generations,
A better earth, a better world,
Not a place where it is difficult to breathe.

Let's learn a lesson from the masters,
The Jesus Christ's, the Buddha's and the Nanaks,
Who talked of love, and peace,
And how to be good humans.

Let's clean up this mess,
I'm sure most of us would agree,
The world could be much better,
If only we could see!

6.

Walk

As I was walking in the park
After so many days
I felt quite free and liberated
As must a prisoner feel when set free

It was wonderful to see so much beauty
If only we could open our eyes to see
And the following thoughts
Came to me

That I can think at all..
Can walk see and hear
That in itself is so fulfilling
Because these treasures will not last

The beautiful sounds of the birds
Amidst the fresh unpolluted air
So many pretty birds
Whose names I don't even know

Many squirrels darting around
Some climbing trees
Others scampering on the ground

Different kinds of flowers
Swaying in the breeze

And in the middle of the green green grass
A bunch of pigeons
Holding a conference
A very fat bird.. Perhaps pregnant

It was wonderful to walk around
And admire in solitude

Two birds swiftly chasing each other
Just like racing cars do
Perhaps they were teenage lovers
Saw a few colorful butterflies too

Another thought came seeing all this beauty
Isn't peace better than war
Why has man not learnt from
History
Didn't the wars bring anything
Other than misery

His story or history now needs to change
And most of us I know feel this way
Let's make our feelings known
So that we can make
A difference or two

7.

Another Day

Another day in life,
Isn't that so nice!
Another chance at happiness,
Of feeling nice and bright!

Another opportunity to set things right,
To introspect,
To feel grateful,
For all the bounties in life.

It feels so good,
To know that all is right,
That there's no need to worry,
For everything will be alright!

As long as we can,
Enjoy the new dawn,
The dusk and the sunset,
The rains and the greenery.

See the perfection,
Of the peas in the pod,

The sweetness of the mango,
The succulent water melon.

The packaging of it all!,
All so naturally!

Have you ever wondered,
At the beauty of the onion,
The taste of the lemon,
The colors in the sky.

The perfect blue,
The scattered white clouds,
The Sun peering through!
Creating shades of various hues.

Nature is Abundant!

You can't fail to notice,
And admire all this beauty,
All of which is gifted,
In every new day!

Thank God for this day,
Or if you don't believe,
You can thank nature too,
It's just a question of belief!

All that is here,
The birds, the bees,
The flowers, the trees,
The different colors.

The beauty of the women,
And the men,
The dogs of various breeds,
Their awesome licks and love!

Isn't all this so magical,
No photograph or painting,
Can match these treasures,
The beauty of the babies!

For some it may just be,
Another dreary day,
But I am sure many would feel,
It's so perfect!! This moment,
And this day!!

8.

Troubled Mind

There is no grammar here..
No full stops or commas..

The path is clear..
It leads straight up..
But there are many diversions..
Along the way to heaven..
Difficult it is.. To overcome the demons.

Easy it is.. To preach..
But very difficult indeed to reach..
Let God give me the strength..
So that I can overcome.

This life is too long..
The woes keep adding up..
As the years go by..
Caused undoubtedly by the Foes..
Those unseen terrible pranksters..
No less than the masked gangsters.

It would be nice..
To be totally occupied..

To think and do right..
Even in the night..
With the help of His might.

The agonies are great..
The nights are long..
When will all this finish..
It seems like eternity.

Let me go now..
If possible without pain..
Not much has been gained..

There is no grammar here..
No full stops or commas.

9.

To Be a Little Boy Once More

How I wish I could go back..
To being a little boy once more..

I was innocent..
I was sweet..
Then I grew up..
And messed up a bit.

I was still innocent.. Most of the time..
Then I grew up more..
And committed some crimes..
Not crimes really..
But some such.. So that it rhymes.

How I wish I could go back..
To be that little boy once more.

And as I grew up more..
Did some more stuff..
Wouldn't be proud to tell..
But I can't hide it.. From myself.

Along with the years..
The follies have only gone up..
More and more..
And now the time has come..
To say.. No more!

So I wish I could go back...
To being that little boy.. Once more

10

Sleep

It is time to sleep now..
And if someone asks..
Do you have any regrets..
My answer would be.. Many..
For I have transgressed..
Many a times..
Succumbed to temptations I have..
But all that has made me what I am..

Life is a journey..
For some it is long..
For me it has been eventful..
I remember all the events..
Not all with pride..
But I have been blessed..
All that I want now..
Is peace in life..
And peace in death.

11.

The Way

Sitting on my bed
Sitting quietly on my bed..
With only thoughts coming in my head..
How much have I traveled..
How far now to go..
I don't know..
I don't know..

What was it that mattered most..
I've seen a lot..
So many downs..
A few ups..
But I'm still there..
Intact..
With my tail up..

I know the secret now..
I will share it with you..
It's just a matter of feeling good..
And it will come.. Only from you

Tell the truth..
Do not pretend..
Be yourself.. No need to impress.
It is just enough to be good.
A good human being..
Not important to be the best.

When I thought there was no escape..
You came and pulled my hand..
I've fallen earlier.. Maybe I will fall again.
But I know you are there.
To pull me through

With this in mind..
I do not want anymore..
I do not need anymore..
Cause I know I'm not alone..
You are there all the time.

So I'm not afraid anymore..
As you are going to be with me..
Even when I'm gone.

12.

The World

What has gone wrong with the world..
Are we so foolish.. To not realize..
There are far more important things to do..
Than make weapons and bombs..
There are so many hungry..
So many crying..
So many thirsty..
So many dying..
So many in pain..

Don't we understand..
What are we trying to do?
Who are we trying to fool..
We buy weapons..
Our neighbours buys weapons..
We buy more weapons..
Where does it all end..
Can't we understand..
Those who are making weapons..
Are just taking us for a ride..
They are not on anyone's side!

Let’s just stop..
No more weapons..
Remove the hunger..
Remove the pain..
Making money..
Is not the only gain.

Have we not learnt..
From all the masters..
Buddha.. Jesus.. Nanak..
All of them preached love..
Not hatred..
Has the world not suffered enough..
The world wars.
The millions who died during partition..
The bombing in Japan.

Come on leaders of the world..
Behave like human beings..
Animals too understand the language of love..
Learn from them.

This life is precious..
No body wants a hero..
With no arms and legs..
Killing and getting killed..
This is stupid!

The times are bad..
People fighting in the name of religion..
Mine is better than yours..
This is the right way to pray..
How does it matter..
Practice religion at your home..
Who cares whether you kneel..
Or stand when you pray..
Become a good human being..
Be a citizen of the world..
Don't be narrow minded..
And throw your rubbish out of the door..

I know there are many who think like me..
And if we all unite..
We can make the world a better place..
There is so much to see..
So much to do..
Enjoy the games..
Play what you like..
See the flowers..
Admire the trees..

We see the same sun..
The same red blood runs through us.
We breathe the same air..

This is a chance. Learn from this pandemic..
There are not enough doctors..
No enough beds..
But there are plenty of weapons..
And bombs in the backyard..
Does it make any sense?

13.

Wake up!!

Before it is too late.
Save the earth.
Save the environment.
Save the fish.
The trees.. The birds..
Save the babies.. And the old men..
Preserve the water..
Spread the love in your heart!

Don't try to prove your strength..
You too will die..
Spread kindness..
Appreciate the wonderful life..
Be grateful..
Do not kill..
Do not harm..
Mend.. Don't break..
Practice.. And don't just preach!!
That's all for now..

14.

The Sun

And the Sun,
Shining silently in the sky,
Has seen it all,
Since the beginning.

When the Sun wasn't there,
There was nothing here,
And when one day,
It came.. That's when it all began.

It must have seen life,
Before the first, man or woman,

When did this happen?
We can only surmise.

Millions of years ago,
When there were fewer men,
And more trees..
Then the rivers were pure.

And then.. Slowly slowly,
Man started wanting,
More and more.

And so slowly.. Slowly,
He started.. This is mine,
And this is mine!
As the Sun.. Watched silently.

More men came,
Then they started to fight,
Started to kill each other.
Feeling very proud of themselves,
Not realising.. They would die too.

Great warriors.. Came and went,
Great explorers.. Came and went,
Religions were formed.
And they started killing,
In the name of God.

The Sun saw it all,
The same Sun.. Shining on all.
Wondering..
Why did I come at all.

And then one day,
People started making territories,
My country is bigger!
My territory is greater!

Man learnt Science,
And more than anything,
Started making weapons,
Making ships and Aeroplanes.

To attack, And conquer and kill.
As the Sun watched silently,
Shining as bright as now,
What are they fighting for.

Slowly, The forests grew less,
The glaciers began to melt,
The rivers got dirty,
Water became less.,
The air became dirty.

The Sun watched,
As man-made bombs,
That could kill millions,
Wondering.. Why did I shine at all.

15.

Tareef

Acchee lagteen hain doston kee tareef..
Dost hain.. Issi liye to..
Karten hain tareef!
Hum ko to itna kuch naheen aata..
Par khuda ka shukr Hai.
Kee dost mil Gaye!

16.

Satisfaction

When are you satisfied?
I guess when you need nothing more,
When are you content?
When you need nothing!

The one who has everything,
And everything has been given free,
Who realises that he or she is nobody,
Then he or she feels satiated.

What did I do,
Nothing really,
And yet... I have more than what I need,
Isn't this amazing.

Is this brain yours?
Or was it given to you,
Are these fingers yours?
With which you type,
Or were they given to you.

The family you were born in,
Did you decide that?

You did not decide your parents!
Your parents did not decide you..

It just happened,
And has kept happening,
Since the ages!!
It's a miracle really!!

That's why now,
I realise,
I am nothing!
And I feel I have got everything!!

17.

Strange

Isn't it strange..
Quite a mystery..
The same person..
How different is he..

Sometimes he is good..
Doing good deeds..
At other times.. So different..
You couldn't even believe.

It's not easy..
This walk of life..
And sometimes..
So pointless it all seems..

What is the reason for coming here..
Is it only a routine..
To pass the days..
To work.. Earn.. Eat..and sleep..
Day after day..

It would be so nice..
If this were more worthwhile..

If being here..
Could add up to some joy..

Strange it is....
The same person..
In front of others..
Shows he is so nice..
But when no one is watching..
Doesn't care a trice.

18.

Confined

Lying in the bed,
Pen in my hand,
A fan whirring on my head,
Scribbling.. Sense or nonsense,
Totally relaxed.. In my pajamas.

Listening to the the sweet sounds,
Of birds.. And the occasional cacophony,
Of the crow,
It's not so bad.. This stay at home.

Peaceful it is here..
Grateful not in some hospital..
All alone.
And whenever I want..
Just get up.. Walk to the kitchen..
Pick up something.. A banana,
Or a snack..
It's not so bad.. This stay at home

Not much to worry about..
No deadlines to meet..
Whenever I want..

Pick up the phone..
And see what's new..
On what's app or Facebook.
It's not so bad.. This stay at home

It's becoming a routine,
Of getting up.. Saying my prayers..
Having breakfast.. Doing the dishes..
Relaxing..
It's not so bad.. This staying at home

Take a bath.. If you want..
No need to rush.. To the car..
No fear of being late to work,
It's not so bad.. Being at home.

I know it will not last..
But best it is..
To make the most of being home.

19.

Sorry

I am sorry
To have hurt you
At times I open my mouth
Without thinking, on the spur of the moment
And then it's too late
To recall what has been said

We have shared more than thirty years
We have each other only
And God knows how many more
We will share together
One of us will go first
Most likely it will be me

I am sorry again
For all the mistakes of the past
I will try
To change my self
So that I don't hurt you
Again

Please do not hold in your heart
Let the past be past

Let each new day
Be a new beginning
Of life more pleasant and joyful

Thank you for tolerating me
I'm glad you are with me
Till my journey lasts

20.

Sona

Aaj Agar neend na bhee aye
To koi baat naheen
Kal to sona hee hai
Umr bhar ke liye

21.

Enjoy the Moments

And now I have decided..
To enjoy the moments..
This God given life..
Is not given to all.

There are all kinds of moments..
Which will come and go..
Some sad.. Some happy..
Some mundane.

But now I realize..
That each day is a blessing..
And a chance..
To improve myself.

To bring joy to others..
Bring changes to yourself..
Be glad of every day..
Even if things are not going your way.

But make the effort..
Think right..
Do the right thing..

For what is most important..
Is peace of mind.

Exercise.. Laugh at yourself..
Make others smile..
Try to learn..
New things.. Every day.

Do not give way to temptations..
They will only make you feel bad..
Those pleasures are very short lived..
Don't do things..
You consider not right..
That will lead you..
Glowing and bright.

Be humble.. Be good..
Don't judge others.. Don't crib..
Don't be jealous..
Accept people.. The way they are.

You know you have too many faults..
No one is all good or bad..
Enjoy this life..
Don't care what people think of you..
Because most of them..
Don't even care.

Don't talk about yourself..
People only get bored..
So don't waste time..
Enjoy this life..
As long as it lasts.

22.

Sin

That feeling of feeling bad..

After you've done something bad
That's a horrible feeling
And it doesn't go away

It stays..
For many years..
And torments..
Perhaps till the end.

It is called remorse..
And there is hardly any cure..

Strength of character lies..
In not succumbing..
But overcoming

Character is..
Not doing something..
Which is oh so sweet..
But is bad..
Even when no one is watching.

That is all there is to it..
To be better.. To be good
The first step is
Not to be bad

You get better..
When you learn to give..
That too.. Without expectation..
That helps.. As you feel
You've done something good

Ultimately you will be judged
By what good you did
Versus the bad
And be sure you will reap
What you sow

That is karma
It is never too late
Nothing is lost
Wake up now!

Rise and shine
Because you know
You are a flower
Even though you have some thorns

23.

Shikayat

Na din Tha.. Na raat thee
Raat woh jo
Beet nahee ho rahi thee
Aur din jo.. Intezar Kara raha tha

Aisa waqt tha
Andhera Tha to sahee
Lekin Ek dhundla saa
Subeh bhee aaney kee koshish me tha

Kya jaaney kab subah hogee
Aur kab laut ayengey woh din
Jab chehrey poorey nazar aatey the

Kya duniya mein keher Kam tha
Jo tumney Ek tufaan bhee bhej diya
Kitnee pariksha logey
Apney bheje huey insaano sey
Kya tumhe accha lagta hai
Agar koi roye?

24.

Reflections - Food on the Table

Food on the table..
A good book to read..
God on my side..
What more can I want

Family members fine..
Friends too in good health..
Even in difficult times..
What more can I want

No cut in electricity..
Internet working fine..
Lying on my bed comfortably..
What more can I want

Water coming in the taps..
No paucity of gas..
Enough stuff in the fridge..
What more can I want

Nice weather..
Good health and sunshine..
No real need to step out..
What more can I want

Praying that the numbers go down..
That a solution is found..
That a lesson is learnt..
By all concerned

Sad to know..
That many are suffering..
Many have died..
Many more will die

But I'm sure..
This too will end..
The cure will be found..
No need to worry.. For God will take care

25

Thoughts on My Life

.. As I reflect.. On my life..
It seems I've wasted a lot of time..
Maybe that's not completely true..
Could have used the time better..
But no point in lamenting now..
.. I'm what I am..
What my thoughts are..
The past can't be erased..
Best to learn from the experience..
The most joys have come from..
Love.. And loving..
Sharing and giving..

26.

Prodigal Son

I can identify with the prodigal son,
I've done all I shouldn't have,
But I'm coming back home again.

And like his father, my Father too,
As is His nature, forgives me,
And welcomes me back, with open arms!

It's a beautiful, joyous homecoming!
It feels good! Just hope I don't stray anymore!

Back home again,
Back home!

27.

God

And when I think of God,
With a pure mind,
A shiver runs from my head,
Into my spine.

I feel His presence,
I know He is there,
He has looked after me till now,
He will do so in the future.

And when He calls me,
I will be happy to go.

He is everywhere,
In everything,
In Living beings,
In places we cannot see,

We cannot know Him,
Our mind is too small,
It is enough to take His name,
And to think of Him.

When He is with us,
Which He is, all the time,
When we feel His presence,
We can do no wrong.

We cannot harm,
We get good thoughts,
We see Him everywhere
In everybody.

We accept whatever happens,
However He keeps us,
Because that's the way,
It was meant to be.

28

Time

Today, let's talk about time,
My time, your time, and time in general.

Time is time, slowly ticking by,
Sometimes ticking fast.
Tick it does, doesn't stop.

Time is timeless,
It's been there, all the time!
It didn't have a beginning,
It doesn't have an end.

It that way, Time and God, well...
In some ways Time is like God,
No beginning, no end!

We are here for a short time,
An instant, in the history of time,
A hundred years, may be less, doubtful more,
We don't really know.

Since we are here for a short time,
Let's make the most of it!
Its very precious, so let's not waste it!

The time gone by, won't come back,
We know that, it's just a memory!

The time to come, we don't know how much,
That's a mystery.
The time now, the present, that's it!
We must enjoy it!

It's great to be sharing this time,
With friends and family and with self..
All the time.

You can't really buy it, this time,
But we spend it, all the time!

At times we don't have a choice,
In spending this limited time,
Like when sent to school, or when in office,
But well, your parents paid for that time,
And your office pays for your time!

And sometimes you have free time!
Enjoy that freedom! In fact, enjoy!
All the time! Even when it is forced on you!
You know it won't last,

Our time will come,
And soon we will be past!

But the journey has been great!
Since infancy till today!
It's time to say bye now,
The clock has ticked by,
Until we meet again,
Till the next time.

29

More Reflections

As I sit and reflect,
Over my life,
A thought comes...
This is accidental. A coincidence!

Our time spent here together,
Sharing all this..
It is divine will!
This family and friends!

All the incidents, the emotions,
The pleasures, pains, excitement
And boredom.
The laughter and the tears!

All this is responsible,
For what we are today.

We of course are not just our bodily form.
Not just what we feel,think and behave.
We are different at different times
Stable in our instability!

It's difficult for anyone to fathom us,
We can't sometimes understand our own self!

But whatever we are,
We are extremely lucky!
To get this human form.
Just wanted to say..
Not all beings are so lucky!!

Let's make the most of it!
Let's explore, experience, enjoy,
Fall and get up! Let's live life,
And be thankful for this wonderful gift!

30

Some More Reflections

Here I am lying on the bed,
Pen in hand and trying to
Conjure thoughts in my head
Life has been very good, I reflect.

Lots of things I have done,
Followed the ten commandments,
I have not.
Done things which shouldn't have been done,
But alas- they can't be undone.

But they have left me wiser,
For now I know,
What gives instant pleasure,
Can turn, to regret, remorse, for a lifetime.

What gives immense peace,
I will share with you,
God forgives all,
If your mind is true.

Give me strength,
So that I remember You,
That fortune and wealth,
Which will stay with you.

It cannot be destroyed,
No one can steal that wealth,
That's the only thing,
That will go with you!

31

Positivity

And as long as I can see..

I will see only the good..
And as long as I can hear..
I will listen.. Only to the true..
And as long as I can feel..
I will feel only the good..
And as long as I can walk..
I will remember.. My good fortune..
That I have the gifts above.

Everything now is a blessing..

Best now.. Is to give..
Things that others can use..
Better than keep..
So that they don't waste away.

Feelings are more important..
Than things..
By sharing..
Will bring true joy and happiness.

So many gifts..
Unopened.. For years..
Are just a waste..
No point.. To accumulate.. And hoard.

The brain and muscles too..
Must be used..
Or else..
Will just waste away.

So remember to exercise..
Don't forget to laugh..
Use your mind..
To fulfill some task.

Spread love..
Make friends.. And keep them..
Look at the positives..
And don't lament

Don't get distracted..
By the noise..
Buy what you want..
But don't waste

Have a balanced life..
Sleep well.. Get up early..
And remember to thank..
For another beautiful day!

32.

No Explanation

Sometimes the thoughts come fast,
And at times they just fly past.

Is there a justification for everything?
Do things happen for a reason?

Many things are beyond explanation,
Science has made a lot of progress,
But still...

Why do things happen the way they do?
Why do people suffer for no apparent fault?

Why are innocent children orphaned?
Why are the poor oppressed?
Why are they poor at all?

Many questions remain unanswered!

It helps to believe that God is there,
That He knows what He is doing,
That ultimately truth and justice will prevail.

What can we do but to accept,
Those who are suffering have to endure,
Why, why do people have to suffer at all!?

We just don't know and can't explain,
It just helps to believe in God!

I have no explanation!

33

While Combing My Hair

This just came
While combing my hair
So quickly took my pen
And wrote away

Some go early some go late
But go we must
That is our fate

But before we go
Make this world
A better place

Be nice be good
Do not worry
Be helpful be kind
Do not cheat
Or harass humankind

Everybody is good
Nobody is bad

God lives in us
As in them

Look at their goodness
Don't criticize
Make this world
A better place

If change you must
Change yourself first
Bring up good children
Teach them well

Be patient with elders
Love the animals
Treat all beings
As your friends

Before we go
Take care of others and yourself
And make this world
A better place!

34

Questions

Do you want recognition,
Do you want acclaim?
Do you want money,
Or do you want fame!

What do you seek,
Are you a seeker?
And more importantly. Are you meek?
Do you want applause
Or do you want peace?

You need to decide what you want,
Then you shall receive!

The truly great,
They never sought fame,
It just came!

They believed in something,
And practised what they preached,
They achieved something great!

Hope to share more thoughts with you,
...soon!

35

Total Peace

And now there is total peace
No need and no greed
Just remembrance and gratitude
I have found the way

I don't know much
But this I know
You give me everything
So there's no fear now

Will try to abandon
Lust, greed, attachment and pride
Once in a while, if I fail too
That's quite alright

He is all knowing, all forgiving
He is my support
He has looked after me thus far
And He will, till the end

True peace I will only find
Once I am gone
I will take with me all my worries
And nothing will bother me
Any more

36.

Peace Of Mind

And now I am at peace..

For somehow I feel..
That God has entered my mind..
So from now on..
I'm just going to follow..
The voice in my head.

I'm going to enjoy the moments..
Whether happy or sad..
Leaving me glad.

Life is beautiful..
Life is precious..
Good food.. Family.. And friends..
So much beauty..
Places of many kinds..

Beautiful songs.. Flowers..
Nice books to read..
Movies to see..
Games to play..
And temples to pray..

Not to forget..
The colorful vegetables..
Licks and kisses..
From the pets.

No more bad thoughts..
No jealousies.. No judging..
No more talking ill
Behind the back.

So I'm Happy now..
It's a decision made..
A resolution..
I shall not break..

Now only to make sure..
To thank God..
For every breath.

37.

Strange Kind of Peace

A strange kind of peace
Comes and resides within me
This is all His grace
Now I have no enemies.. Only friends

Quite content.. With all that He has given
For it is more.. Much more
Than I deserved or expected

Now all that I need to
Is to remember Him all the time
So that I don't do anything
Which is not right

38.

Came with Nothing

You came with nothing
You will go with nothing
In between
You did or will do something

Did what you do or will
Count for anything
Or was it just nothing
Did it make life better for anyone

Did it make life better
For you or anyone
If not, then it means nothing
Try and do something
Before you become nothing

Do some good for yourself
By doing good for others
If nothing else bring some joy
Some smiles to others and self

Let people feel
He did something worthwhile

Something which helped
To make this beautiful world
A little better

For you came with nothing
And you will go with nothing
But you can be glad
That in between
You did some good some things

39.

Over the Years

Over the years,
I have accumulated,
Many memories, and some trash,
Some possessions and a little cash.

Made some friends,
Enjoyed a lot,
Sometimes was distressed,
But that time passed.

I just want to enjoy, this beautiful God given gift,
Fill it with pleasant thoughts and love,
Erase all the bad moments of the past.

Bear no ill will to anyone,
No jealousy, no hatred or anger,
No finding faults,
As I have so many of my own.

When in an argument,
It's better to lose,
Rather than to bring any misery,
By proving you are right.

Penning my thoughts,
As they come,
Trying to catch some good ones,
Before they are dropped!
Sharing them,
For whatever they are worth,
Perhaps my feelings,
Might strike a chord!

40.

Clinging

I am in the habit of clinging
Clinging to things..
Also clinging to the past
The time has come
To uncling!

The cupboards are full of old things
Old notes..clothes..even pens!
The mind is full of the past..
The time has come..
To make some space..

Best it is to give..
If of use to someone
Else...just discard..
Make some space

Empty yourself of the useless
Make space for the useful
You can't carry anything
Don't leave your possessions
For others to sort and discard

41.

Shayar

Ab chain kee neend kahan aati
Subeh uthna ka
To ik bahana sa ho gaya
Is lock down ney to
Mujh jaise ko bhee
Shayar Bana diya!

42.

Neend Khul Gayi

Jab mein utha, Ek lambee neend sey,
To sab kuch accha lagney laga,
Jin cheezon pey dhyan kabhi nahee Para,
Ab unko ascharya sey dekhne laga,
Ye pattey, kitney sunder Hain,
Ye phool kitney khoobsoorat Hain,
Yeh perh.. Sunderta chidiya or gilehree
Mein nazar aaney lagee..
Poora nazariya hee badal gaya..
Zindagee khubsoorat lagney lagi..
Chand ko dekhtey achha lagta Hai Ab..
Har din ka ehsaas hota Hai..
Bhagwan kee yaad aatee Hai.. Aur
Bahut shukr karney laga..
Kitnee gift mileen Hain..
Aankhen.. Paer, mukh ka swaad.. Sab kuch diya Hai..
Aur jab inmey kuch bhee takleef hoti Hai.. Tab inkee keemat maloom padti Hai... Let us be grateful.. For all that we have got for free!! The things which are priceless.. We have got free!!

43.

Name and Fame

Some achieve notoriety,
Some achieve fame,
But there are lots of good people,
Who don't get a name!

It doesn't really matter,
Whether you are known or not,
What matters is that you have,
Some special persons,
Who will always care.

Whether you are on social media,
Five friends or five thousand,
Zero likes or in hundreds,
Does anyone really care?

Ultimately it won't matter,
And neither will we,
As we too are matter,
And dust we shall be.

While we have this beautiful life,
Spend more time with those who are precious,

For the rest of them,
Don't matter much at all.

If you are the religious type,
Then believe in your religion,
Practice what it says,
All religions tell you,
Speak the truth and be good.
Isn't that what they all preach.

And if you don't believe in God,
Or you're not quite sure,
That's very well too,
As long as you keep your word,
And are being human too!

Perhaps I preach too much,
But this is what I believe,
A happy person is good,
And a good person will be happy!

44.

My Own Best Friend

I am my own best friend
I know I have only me
My parents cared
But they are not there now

All others, companions, friends,
Relatives and family.
Are there, but cannot be there
All the time

I have realised
That basically I am on my own
Thus I cease to have
Undue expectations

Whatever love I receive
Is purely a bonus
I need to love myself
And be happy with myself

I am all the time with myself
More so when I am alone
And I say this without regret
I like myself and
I am perfectly OK to be my own best friend!

45.

Morning

It's a beautiful morn,
The birds whistling,
At the crack of dawn,
The air fresh and pure!
As if the past misdeeds,
Have been washed away!
The leaves on the trees,
Begin to sway.

A gentle breeze,
Kisses my cheeks,
I look up and see,
The unpolluted sky!

All is well,
It's a new beginning,
A new opportunity,
A wish for peace,
And an end to the disease.

It's a daily gift,
This freshness of dawn,

Don't take it for granted,
Enjoy while you can.

One of these days,
You will not be able to see,
The daily miracle,
So enjoy while you can,
Before the darkness,
Comes your way.

46.

Way of Life

Good it is to be detached,
Even better to be content,
Best to accept.

When,how and where,
The wind blows,
Its not in your hands.

Good or bad,you decide,
Let others decide,
For themselves.

Don't judge,
Or criticize,
It doesn't help.

For me what works,
Is belief,
Remembrance and gratitude.

I don't expect,
And when i get,
Thats good.

Now i am at peace,
And there is no reason,
Why this should change.

This way works for me,
And i wish,
Peace for you as well.

47.

Ending and Before That

Is it the end,
Or simply a new beginning,
We all know,
The soul doesn't die.

The body out of breath,
Will perish,
But so what,
In any case with age,
It does shrivel.
The brown leaf falls,
And a new fresh green leaf emerges
Thats all!

Look at the positive side of everything,
Even death,
For all the worries and pain,
Will go away.

It will be a deep sleep,
Without dreams,
And there will be total peace.

No one's words, deeds,
Could affect you,
Sorrow could not touch you.

But till it comes,
The most important thing,
Enjoy, be joyful, laugh like a child!
Don't worry, for you know,
Nothing is in your hands,
You are not the doer, He is!

And once you realize,
It's all in His hands,
Just see,
All things are sorted,
Everything comes in place.

Even if there is pain or suffering,
It is momentary,
And part of His gift,
Only so that when it is gone,
You can appreciate,
Your wellbeing even more!

From your side,
Decide for yourself,
What you think is right and wrong,
And try and do more right than wrong!

You are bound to slip,
Once in a while,
As you are only human,
And you are bound to err!

But you know also,
That He is ever forgiving,
And will reward you,
When you resist the temptations.

These are my thoughts,
I will share them with you,
If you like them,
Do give your feedback,
If you don't, that's OK too!

48.

Life-like a River

Life
Just like the journey of a drop,
In the river,
Which merges into the sea,
We too will merge, into the earth.

And like the drop,
Which comes back again,
From vapor to rain,
From the dust, we might emerge,
In a different shape.

Like the water,
Life will flow,
Sometimes fast, sometimes slow,
Flow it will, till it turns to dust.

Enjoy the journey,
Don't worry at all,
No one is perfect,
Nothing will last.

The pain won't last,
Nor will the pleasure,
Build good memories,
Of the past.

We all are different, yet alike,
We share this journey,
Isn't that nice!

What good is hatred,
What good is anger,
What good is jealousy,
What good is pride.

All this, including lust,
Will only eat you away,
And leave you empty.

Fill your life with love,
With compassion, with patience,
Be happy yourself, and spread it,
It will only increase.

Let people remember you,
For your good, for your smiles,
For the love you spread.

This is the essence,
Of what I have learnt,

The good you do,
Will come back to you
The bad you do,
Will only torment you.

Enjoy the journey,
Don't worry at all,
Life and death,
Are just two sides of the coin,
After all.

49.

Meant to be

Where I am today,
Is what was meant to be,
Don't think for a moment,
That it was something you did..
Which made you what you are.

This was all planned,
Right from the beginning,
Even before you were born,
He already had a plan.

You have only one thing,
Which you must try to do,
Listen to the voice in your head
Which was put inside you.

If you listen,
You will be fine,
You will be on the right path,
If you don't, you will pay the price.
But don't worry, it's all a learning,
Its all taken care of!

So go and do your thing,
Enjoy,Laugh,play,have fun,
Do good, be good, trust people,
There is nothing that can happen,
Which is not meant to be!

Just try and remember,
To listen,
To the voice in your head,
And be carefree!

50.

Is Man Intelligent

Is Man Intelligent
Is man intelligent?
I don't know.

After so much history,
So many wars,
He still hasn't learnt.

Still talks in terms of mine!
My country! My religion!

And so all 200 plus countries,
Have their own army, weapons.

People in the world still don't have clean
drinking water!

It's a shame,
Resources are being wasted!

Sophisticated weapons, unmanned drones,
Nuclear weapons, chemical weapons,
Missiles, you name it! They are all there!

They don't realize...
This world is unique,
The only heavenly body amongst millions,
Which has life!

Yet we delight in weapons of destruction!

Most people I know,
Will agree with me,
Let's stop this foolishness!
Let's become wise!
Let's grow up,
Let's be mature!
Let's work for a better world,
A safer place,
For the generations to come!

Let's fight the other big problems! Disease,
Environment, global warming, lack of education, etc
Unitedly!!

51.

Burden

Burden
He walked slowly,
With his heavy burden of sins,
Which only increased,
As life went on.

He knew,
The end has to come one day,
Perhaps nearer now,
Rather than far.

Would the sins burn too,
With the body?
I know I won't feel a thing,
When it burns,
But now, while there are breaths,
It surely hurts!

The only way,
To lessen the burden,
Is two pronged,
Not to increase the sins,
And try and do some good instead!

The path is clear,
The destination is near,
And now is the time to act!
Before it is too late.

52.

Memories

Memories are all I have,
Good memories, bad memories,
Happy memories, sad memories,
Memories of people who made me happy,
Memories of those who took care,
Memories of those who stood by me,
Who accepted me, who gave me love,
Some memories I would like to erase,
But the button just isn't there,
Maybe it's so, to make me understand,
Don't create more which will increase the hurt.

But apart from memories,
I have thoughts too,
And I'm happy to say,
Most are good!

When it's time to go,
The property and money won't matter,
The memories and thoughts,
And loved ones by your side,
Will ease the way,
From this world to the next.

I just want to say to you my friend,
I love you in a special way.

The ending of this poem,
Is a little disjointed,
But it doesn't matter,
I'm not perfect and won't ever be,
Errors do creep in,
That's how it is meant to be!

53.

Meditation

It is 5 in the morning..
And as I try to meditate..
But the sweet sounding..
Chirps of the birds..
Make me hesitate.

Waheguru.. Waheguru.. I try to do..
And the birds continue.. With their
Chirping too..
Perhaps they in their own way..
Are meditating too!

Welcoming a new day..
Delighted at being alive..
Thinking and listening..
To the sounds of God

And then a mosquito arrives..
With a clap.. I try..
To squash it..
Don't succeed..
Perhaps it is doing..
It's thing too!

So this is life..
The birds are there..
Sweet sounding and pretty..
But so are the mosquitoes..
Ugly and irritating.

It is upto us..
To choose to ignore..
The mosquitoes..
And to listen to the birds..
And the sound of God.. within.

The mosquito tries again..
To land a bite.. On my hand..
But by now.. I have picked up my pen
And choose to ignore..

He has made..
All kinds of creatures..
Including us..
It is upto us..
To choose.. What should affect us..
If at all.

The TV is on too..
The sweet sounds of kirtan..
Float in the air..
So this is life..

Full of all things.. Thoughts..
And distractions.

In fact.. Life is..
Quite like a poetry..
It has a beginning..
Some good.. Some bad..
Some quite ordinary..
Some sad
And it has to end..
Like this poetry too.

54.

Marzee

Sooraj jab apnee ankh kholega
To usko bahut sey log
Ghabraye hue nazar ayenge
Kuch gharon key andar
Aur kuch bahar nakaab mein.

Yeh kaisi zindagi ho gayi hai
Jo zindagi kee uthal puthal
Achanak band ho gayi Hai!

Kya yeh cheen ney kiya
Ya Kissi insaan ney
Mujhey to itna Pata hai
Tumhari marzee ke bina
Ek patta bhee nahi hilta
To yeh sab Tumhari marzee hai
Kee Hum sabak seekh jayen
Zindagi kaise jeetey hain
Iska sahi maina seekh jayen
Jahan sabhi jeevon kee
Kadar ho
Sirf insaan apnee na chalaye
Aur insaaniyat ka Matlab samajh Jaye!

55

The Game of Life

Some go early,
Some go late,
Some go all of a sudden,
Some just linger on.

It is not in our hands,
So there's no need to care,
Best it is to live fully each day,
What we do today,
Will be a sweet memory of tomorrow.

Everything has a positive side,
Even death,
That's, an end to the worry and the pain,
It is sad to lose a near one,
What can we do,
We have to accept.

What happens is part karma,
Past and present they say,
It's a matter of His will and grace,
Perhaps bad karma, the good will erase.

We are just blessed that we came,
In the first place,
Lucky to be born as humans,
And not an insect or a snake.

It has its miseries and pain,
But more than that,
There is so much joy and beauty,
Just open your heart and see.

Ride the bicycle of life,
We will get punctures,
Along the way,
The brake may fail,
We might fall down.

But it's a lovely journey,
And covers many miles,
Make it full of smiles,
Theres a lot to be grateful for!

I will end now,
With my two pieces of advice,
Love all! Come let's play,
Some we will win and some lose,
But isn't it a pleasure playing,
This game of life!

56.

What is Life

What is life to me?
Life means to live,
Life means to be happy,
Life means to care and share.

Life means to learn,
Life means to earn,
Life means to love,
Life means having no regrets!

Life means to enjoy,
Life means to play,
Life means to eat good food,
Life means to make friends.

Life means to respect,
Life means to forgive,
Life means to move on,
Life means to give.

Life is wonderful!
Life means to be aware,
Life means to enjoy the beauty.

Life is full of experiences,
Life is a bundle of memories.

Life has its moments,
We all have this one life,
It means our time here,
Life means keeping this place beautiful.

Life means adding to the joy,
Life is enjoying ice cream!
Life is playing with a toy,
Let's add to the joy.

Life becomes worthwhile,
If you can get someone to smile,
Life means being at peace,
Life means being true.

Life means trusting,
Life means giving each other space,
Life means being carefree,
Life means listening to a nice song.

Life has sadness too,
It's OK to cry,
Once in a while.

Life means being simple and honest,
Life means being grateful,

Life means not wasting time,
Life is beautiful!

Life means to appreciate,
Life means not finding faults,
Life means not being petty,
Life means acceptance and gratitude.

Life means fighting injustice,
Life means being nice to people,
Life means respecting everybody.

Life means being able to say no,
Life means not allowing someone
To tread on your toe.

Life means looking after your health,
Life means not being proud of your wealth.
Life means not being short of breath!
Life means enjoying with friends,
Life is playing with a puppy,
Life means holding a baby.

Life means doing good deeds,
And having good thoughts,
Life means taking things in your stride,
Life means having no pride.

Life means loving your family,
Life means to adjust,
Life means not being selfish,
Life means having a caring wife,
Life means having a few who love.

Life is a precious gift,
So enjoy this present,
And live in the present moment,
Life means just life,
And all that's nice!

This is what life means to me,
Life is a gift.. And I'm going to make the most of it!

Life means everything,
Most of all,
Life gets a meaning,
When we remember Him.

57.

What Does It Mean for Me

This is what I wrote.. For myself..

Perhaps this is what I want to be.. Maybe it's me.. Just some thoughts.. Not a poetry..

So here goes...

Enjoy the moments..
Whether good or bad..
Whether pleasure or pain..
Be sure they won't last

Life is made up of moments..
Be in the moment..
If you are having tea..
Enjoy it.. Savour it.
If you are talking to someone..
Or listening..
Give them your undivided attention.

Respect every one..
Respect everything..
You are where you are..
Not because of anything you did..
It was just chance..

You were born where you were..
That was not in your hands..
So empathize..
You could have been the beggar in the streets..
Or the security guard at the office..
So talk to them nicely.

Don't get affected by how people talk to you..
Some in position of authority may shout..
But don't let it affect you

Some who love you..
Also may talk badly..
Just don't have any expectations..
Let your peace not get disturbed..
Don't give anyone..the power to affect your
happiness..

I don't care if you or anyone has two cars or six..
A big or a small house..
What is important is how these people behave..
How they talk to people..
Especially those less privileged than them..

Money is not bad..
But remember money is not the most important thing..
Some of the best things come free..
Love.. Respect.. Fresh air.. A smile..
More important is your love..
How you treat your elders..
Whether you are kind to little children.

Try giving..
If not money.. Give your time..
Or your smile..
And remember to be grateful..
You have got both eyes..
You can hear properly..
Not everyone has those..
Or a pretty nose!

You get food every day..
You have a home..
You have a car..
A child.. And a job..
So thank Almighty for His blessings..

Not everyone is as fortunate..
Remember life is temporary..
So enjoy it..
It won't last..
Nothing will..

So be happy..
Don't worry..
Your fate was decided..
Even before you were born..

But always listen to your inner self..
Your conscience..
As you know yourself..
Better than anyone else..

No one will know your sins or crimes..
Even if no one knows..
You know what you did..
And you can't escape from it..
You can never get over the guilt..

So be intelligent..
Be far sighted..
Don't give away to momentary..
Temptation..

If you learn to think of others..
That will give you the biggest joy..
So enjoy this beautiful gift..

Remember.. Who are you to give..
You.. You have been given everything..
What you have got..

Remember it's not because of your efforts..
It's a gift.

But of course..
Make the effort..
Enjoy your work..
Enjoy the company of your friends..
Your family.. Especially elderly people..
And little children..
Remember that children are..
The most pure..

Help people..
Not with the expectation of getting..
Anything back..
But because you will enjoy..
Doing a good deed..

Make friends..
Most people in the world are nice..
It's just that you haven't connected..

Don't judge..
Who are you to judge..
You've done enough bad yourself..
So think.. Look at yourself first..
Before pointing fingers.

Stay away from negativity..
People who find fault with everything..
Who think too much about themselves..
Who keep boasting..
The overbearing and the bullies..

Enjoy the jokes..
Enjoy your own stupidity..
Laugh at yourself..

Enjoy reading..
Enjoy learning..
Listen more than you speak..

Take time to be with yourself..
Love yourself..
Only then will you radiate..
The love within.

Make someone happy..
But stick to your principles..
Do things you've never done..
Cooking.. Take up a hobby..
Gardening or music..
Learn a new language.

Subdue your ego..
Know that essentially you are a nobody..

There are many who are better than you..
You are not good.. And nobody is bad..

Be happy and content..
Know that all is in the will of God..
So accept all times..
As His grace.. Whether good or bad.

That's all for now!!

58.

Leaves

The leaves baked by the sun..
Fall to the earth..
Because their time has come..

They have seen it all..
The different seasons..
The winter.. Summer and fall..

New leaves will come..
They will grow..
They too will fall..

59.

Know Yourself

And you know yourself..
Better than anybody else..
So what matters is.
What you think of yourself..

What good have you done..
What bad..
Which lies have you told..
Whom have you put down..
So wake up now..
Time is short..
Get up!

60.

Just Enough

To be happy you don't need much

You need just enough!

If you get everything on a platter
You don't value it much
If you earn yourself
And buy, you feel pride and value it much

To be happy you don't need much
You need just enough

You need good health for which
Exercise, laughter good sleep is enough
Fancy cars and watches
Don't matter too much

We see plenty of brats
In fancy cars and blaring music
Blowing up their parents money
Are they or their parents happy?
Haven't they had enough!

Happy are those
Who toil hard and come home tired
And enjoy a meal with wife and family
Because that's quite enough

Keep it simple
Look after your mind and body
Invest in your self, your character
That's more than enough

Remember that you are just a drop
In the ocean or a grain of sand
In the desert
Don't ever think that you are
Too much

Remember God
Be grateful
Open your eyes
To the joys of the world
And thank God for giving you
Just enough!

9 788197 770296

Printed at Repro India Ltd.